# BOOK ONE 1

# POPULAR PIANO SOLOS

# JOHN THOMPSON'S
## ADULT PIANO COURSE

The price of this publication includes access to audio and MIDI tracks online
for download or streaming, using the unique code below.

To access audio visit:
www.halleonard.com/mylibrary

Enter Code
5858-2135-9644-2179

ISBN 978-1-4803-6745-6

Exclusively Distributed By

WILLIS MUSIC

HAL•LEONARD®
CORPORATION
7777 W. BLUEMOUND RD. P.O. BOX 13819
MILWAUKEE, WISCONSIN 53213

Visit Hal Leonard Online at
www.halleonard.com

The popular songs in this collection were arranged and edited with the adult student in mind. They are perfectly suited to the student learning from *John Thompson's Adult Piano Course* (Book 1), but are also appropriate for students learning from any method, or for anyone playing the piano for personal pleasure and enjoyment.

# CONTENTS

# Sweet Caroline

With *John Thompson's Adult Piano Course (Book 1)*, use after page 9.

Words and Music by
Neil Diamond
Arranged by Carolyn Miller

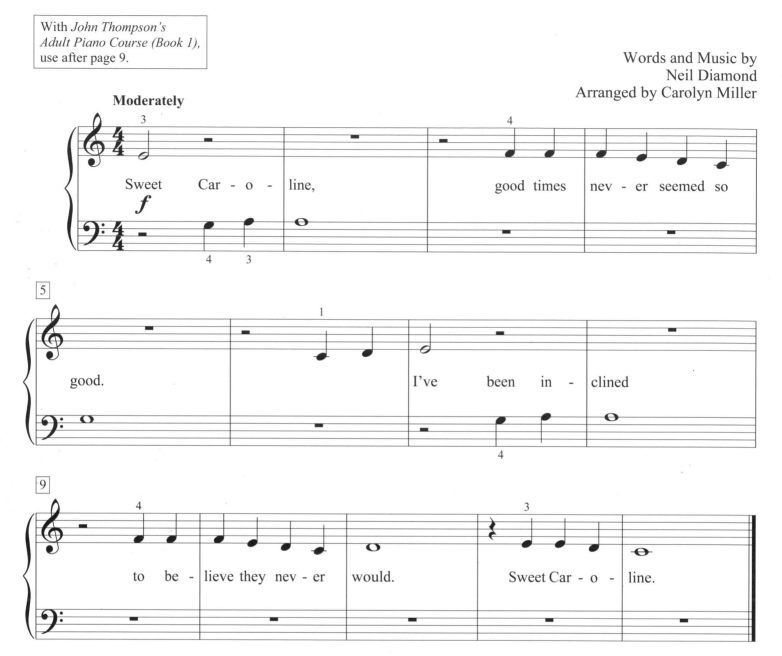

**Accompaniment** (Student plays one octave higher than written.)

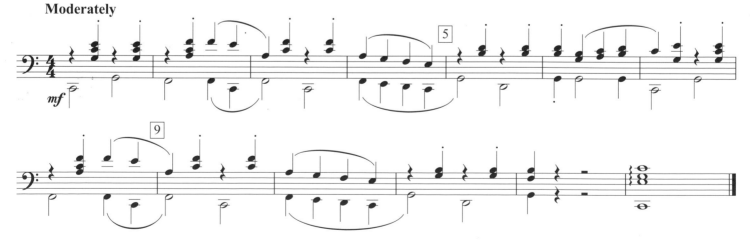

# Can't Help Falling in Love

from the Paramount Picture BLUE HAWAII

Use after page 11.

Words and Music by George David Weiss,
Hugo Peretti and Luigi Creatore
Arranged by Carolyn Miller

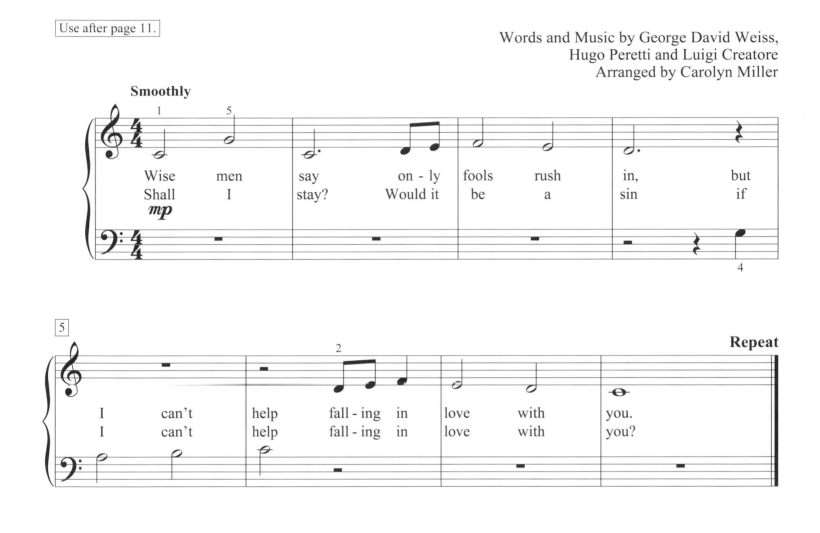

# Born Free

from the Columbia Pictures' Release BORN FREE

Use after page 13.

Words by Don Black
Music by John Barry
Arranged by Carolyn Miller

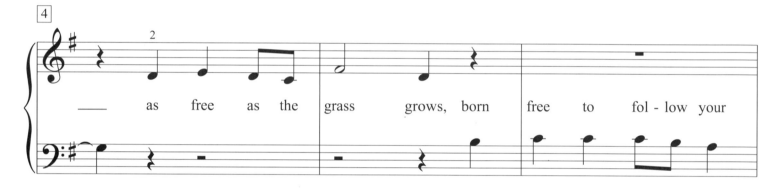

**Accompaniment** (Student plays one octave higher than written.)

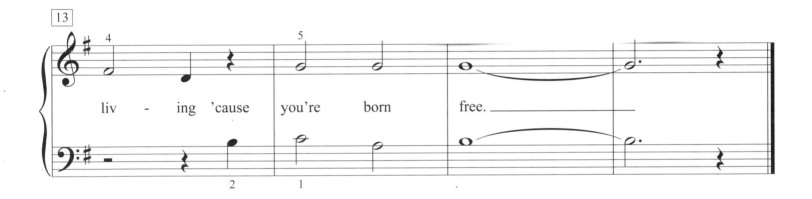

# Fields of Gold

Use after page 15.

Music and Lyrics by Sting
Arranged by Carolyn Miller

You'll re - mem - ber me    when the    west wind moves    a - mong the fields    of

bar - ley.    You can    tell    the sun    in his    jeal - ous sky    as we

**Repeat**

walk    in    fields    of    gold,    when we    walk    in    fields    of    gold.

**Accompaniment** (Student plays one octave higher than written.)

# Every Breath You Take

Use after page 23.

Music and Lyrics by Sting
Arranged by Carolyn Miller

**Moderate Rock**

Ev-'ry breath you _ take, ev-'ry move you _ make,

ev-'ry bond you break, ev-'ry step you take, I'll be watch-ing you.

Ev-'ry sin - gle _ day, ev-'ry word you _ say,

ev-'ry game you play, ev-'ry night you stay, I'll be watch-ing you. _____

# Ob-La-Di, Ob-La-Da

Use after page 38.

Words and Music by John Lennon
and Paul McCartney
Arranged by Carolyn Miller

*Bring out the left hand melody*

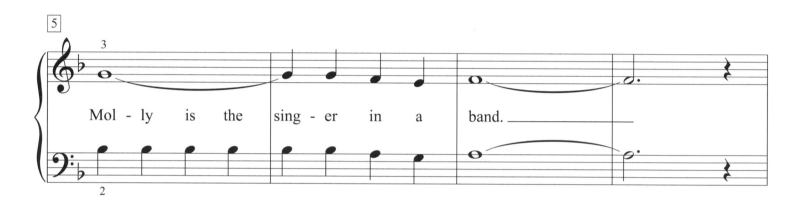

# My Life

Use after page 32.

Words and Music by
Billy Joel
Arranged by Carolyn Miller

Moderato

I don't need ___ you to wor - ry for me ___'cause I'm all right.

I don't want ___ you to tell ___ me it's time ___ to come home.

I don't care ___ what you say ___ an - y - more, ___ this is my life.

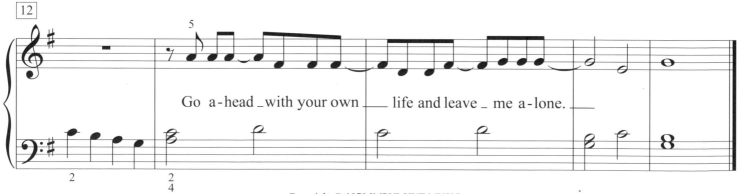

Go a-head ___with your own ___ life and leave ___ me a-lone.

# Open Arms

Use after page 45.

Words and Music by Steve Perry
and Jonathan Cain
Arranged by Carolyn Miller

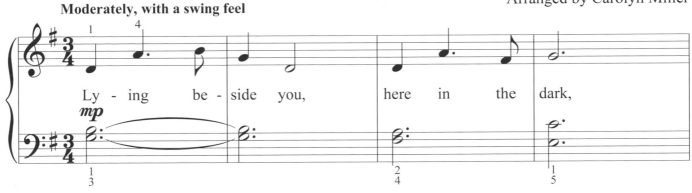

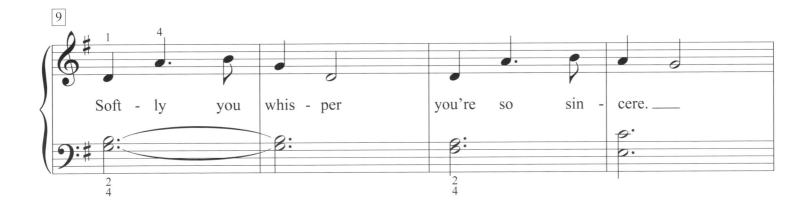

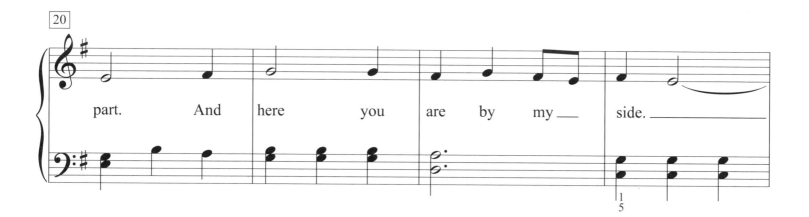

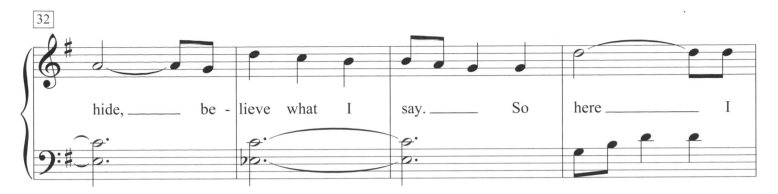

hide, \_\_\_\_\_ be - lieve what I say. \_\_\_\_\_ So here _____ I

am _____ with o - pen arms, \_\_\_\_\_ hop - ing you'll

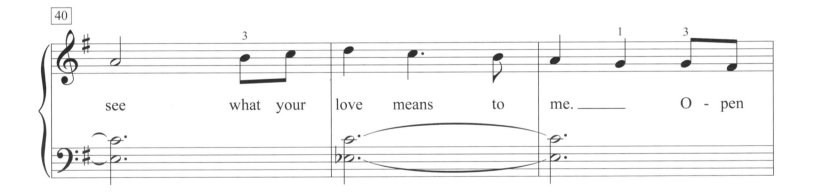

see what your love means to me. \_\_\_\_\_ O - pen

arms. _____ *rit.*

# Raindrops Keep Fallin' on My Head

## from BUTCH CASSIDY AND THE SUNDANCE KID

Lyric by Hal David
Music by Burt Bacharach
Arranged by Carolyn Miller

Use after page 56.

**With a little swing**

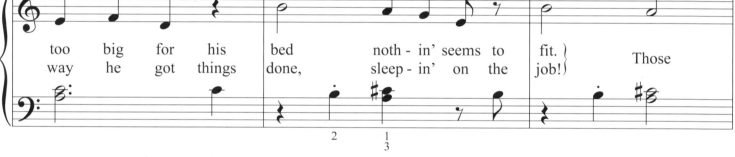

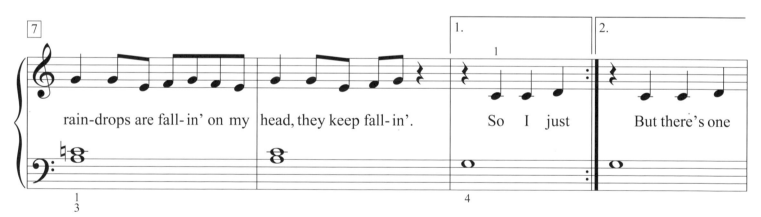

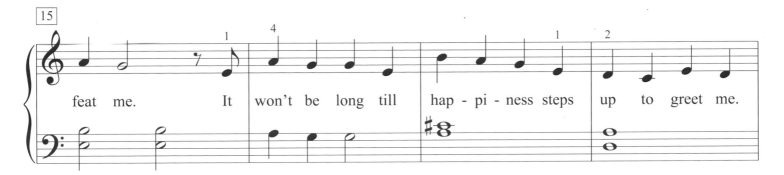

feat me. It won't be long till hap - pi - ness steps up to greet me.

Rain - drops keep fall - in' on my head, but

that does-n't mean my eyes will soon be turn - in' red. Cry-in's not for

me 'cause I'm nev - er gon - na stop the rain by com-plain-in'.

Be - cause I'm free noth-in's wor-ry - in' me. _____

# Give My Regards to Broadway

from LITTLE JOHNNY JONES

Use after page 63.

Tip:

Words and Music by
George M. Cohan
Arranged by Carolyn Miller

Give my re - gards to Broad - way, re -

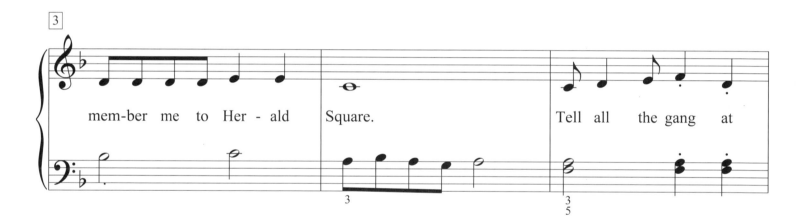

mem-ber me to Her - ald Square. Tell all the gang at

For - ty - sec - ond Street that I will soon be there.

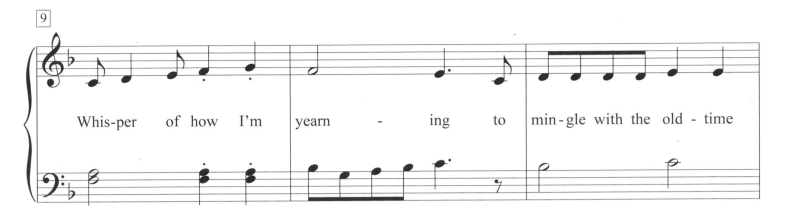

9

Whis-per    of  how  I'm    yearn  -  ing    to    min - gle  with  the  old - time

12

throng.    Give my  re - gards  to    old  Broad - way  and  say  that

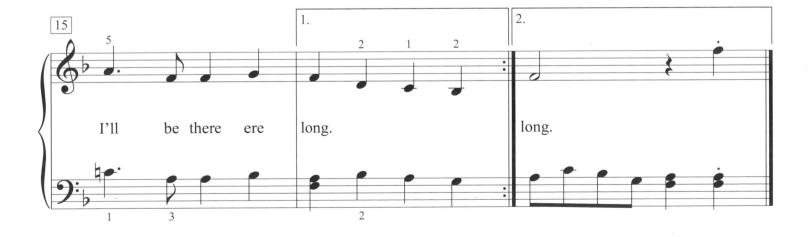

15

I'll    be  there  ere    long.                long.

# A Groovy Kind of Love

Use after page 66.

Words and Music by Toni Wine
and Carole Bayer Sager
Arranged by Carolyn Miller

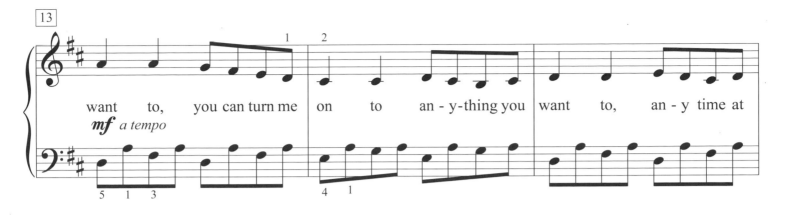

# Rainy Days and Mondays

Use after page 79.

Lyrics by Paul Williams
Music by Roger Nichols
Arranged by Carolyn Miller

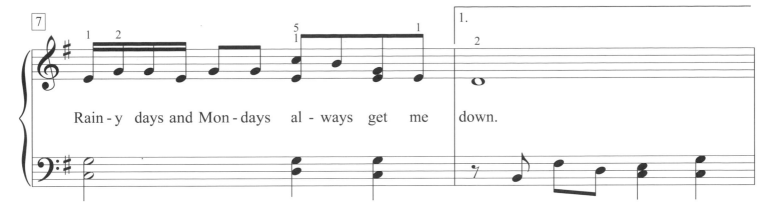

Rain - y days and Mon - days al - ways get me down.

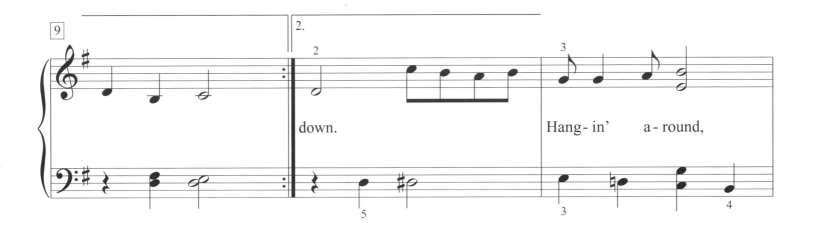

down.  Hang - in' a - round,

noth - in' to do but frown.  Rain - y days and Mon - days al - ways

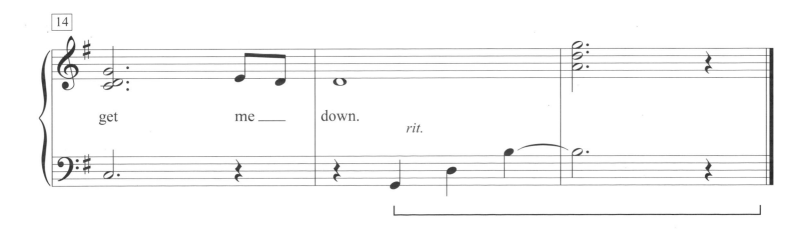

get me down.  *rit.*

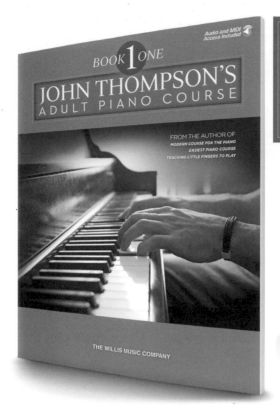

# REDISCOVER
## JOHN THOMPSON'S
### ADULT PIANO COURSE

### ADULT PIANO COURSE

Recently re-engraved and updated, *John Thompson's Adult Piano Course* was compiled with the mature student in mind. Adults have the same musical road to travel as the younger student, but the study material for mature students will differ slightly in content. Since these beloved books were written and arranged especially for adults, they contain a wonderful mix of classical arrangements, well-known folk-tunes and outstanding originals that many will find a pleasure to learn and play. Most importantly, the student is always encouraged to play as artistically and with as much musical understanding as possible. Access to orchestrations online is available and features two tracks for each piece: a demo track with the piano part, and one with just the accompaniment.

| | | |
|---|---|---|
| 00122297 | Book 1 – Book/Online Audio | $14.99 |
| 00412639 | Book 1 – Book Only | $6.99 |
| 00122300 | Book 2 – Book/Online Audio | $14.99 |
| 00415763 | Book 2 – Book Only | $6.99 |

---

### POPULAR PIANO SOLOS – JOHN THOMPSON'S ADULT PIANO COURSE

12 great arrangements that can be used on their own, or as a supplement to *John Thompson's Adult Piano Course*. Each book includes access to audio tracks online that be downloaded or streamed.

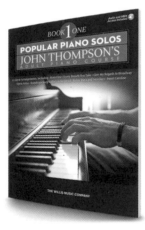

### BOOK 1

*arr. Carolyn Miller*

Born Free • Can't Help Falling in Love • Every Breath You Take • Fields of Gold • Give My Regards to Broadway • A Groovy Kind of Love • My Life • Ob-La-Di, Ob-La-Da • Open Arms • Raindrops Keep Fallin' on My Head • Rainy Days and Mondays • Sweet Caroline.

**00124215 Book/Online Audio $12.99**

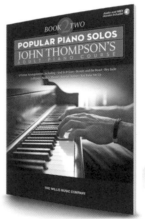

### BOOK 2

*arr. Eric Baumgartner & Glenda Austin*

And So It Goes • Beauty and the Beast • Getting to Know You • Hey Jude • If My Friends Could See Me Now • Lollipop • My Favorite Things • Nadia's Theme • Strawberry Fields Forever • Sunrise, Sunset • Sway (Quien Será) • You Raise Me Up.

**00124216 Book/Online Audio $12.99**

---

### Also Available, JOHN THOMPSON RECITAL SERIES:

### SPIRITUALS
*Intermediate to Advanced Level*

Six excellent arrangements that are ideal for recital or church service. Titles: Deep River • Heav'n, Heav'n • I Want to Be Ready (Walk in Jerusalem, Jus' like John) • Nobody Knows De Trouble I've Seen • Short'nin' Bread • Swing Low, Sweet Chariot.

00137218 .............................. $6.99

### THEME AND VARIATIONS
*Intermediate to Advanced Level*

Fantastic recital variations that are sure to impress: Chopsticks • Variations on Mary Had a Little Lamb • Variations on Chopin's C Minor Prelude • Three Blind Mice - Variations on the Theme • Variations on Twinkle, Twinkle, Little Star.

00137219.............................. $8.99

### WALTZES
*Intermediate to Advanced Level*

Excellent, virtuosic arrangements of famous romantic waltzes: Artist's Life (Strauss) • Paraphrase on the Beautiful Blue Danube (Strauss) • Dark Eyes (Russian Cabaret Song) • Vienna Life (Strauss) • Waltz of the Flowers (Tchaikovsky) • Wedding of the Winds (John T. Hall).

00137220.............................. $8.99

Prices, contents, and availability subject to change without notice.